NFT

Getting rich in a fast forward reshaping economy

1 PREFACE

Over the past few years, non-fungible tokens (NFTs) have exploded onto the scene, transforming the way we think about digital art, collectibles, and ownership. NFTs are unique digital assets that are recorded on a blockchain, and they are being used to represent everything from digital art and music to virtual real estate and collectibles.

As the popularity of NFTs continues to grow, it is important to understand what they are and how they work. This book provides a comprehensive overview of NFTs, including their history, technical foundations, and applications in various industries.

Throughout the book, you will learn about the key features of NFTs, including their unique identity, ownership, and scarcity. You will also explore the various platforms and technologies that are being used to create and sell NFTs, and the legal and ethical issues that surround their use.

So, if you are ready to dive into the world of NFTs, let's get started!

2 DEFINITIONS:

2.1 NFTs

Non-Fungible Tokens, or NFTs, are digital assets that use blockchain technology to prove ownership and authenticity. NFTs are unique, meaning that they cannot be replaced or exchanged for something else of equal value. This makes them highly prized by collectors and investors to own rare and valuable digital items.

NFTs were first introduced in 2017 with the launch of the Ethereum blockchain, which made it possible to create and trade unique digital assets. Since then, NFTs have gained widespread popularity and have been used to represent a wide range of digital items, including art, music, videos, and even tweets.

One of the key features of NFTs is that they are stored on a decentralized database, which means that they are not controlled by any single person or organization. This makes them resistant to censorship and allows for an important level of transparency and security.

The value of an NFT is determined by a variety of factors, including the rarity and uniqueness of the digital asset, the reputation and fame of the creator, and the demand from collectors and investors. Some NFTs have sold for millions of dollars, making them some of the most valuable digital assets in the world.

One of the most well-known examples of an NFT is the "CryptoKitties" game, which allows players to breed, collect, and trade unique digital cats. The game became a phenomenon in the NFT space, with some of the rarest cats selling for hundreds of thousands of dollars.

Another example of NFTs is the art world, where digital art has gained increasing recognition and value. Many artists have started using NFTs to sell and showcase their work, and some have achieved tremendous success and fame as a result. One notable example is the artist Beeple, whose digital artwork has sold for millions of dollars at auction.

Despite the growing popularity and success of NFTs, there are also some concerns and criticisms surrounding their use. One concern is that NFTs may contribute to the growing divide between the rich and the poor, as they are often only accessible to those who can afford to pay unaffordable prices for them. There are also concerns about the environmental impact of the blockchain technology used to create and trade NFTs, as it requires a large amount of energy to operate.

Overall, NFTs represent a new and exciting development in the world of digital assets, and they have the potential to revolutionize the way we think about ownership and value in the digital realm. However, it is important to consider the potential consequences and limitations of this technology as it continues to evolve.

2.2 BLOCKCHAIN

Blockchain technology is a decentralized database that allows for the secure and transparent tracking of transactions. It is a distributed ledger that is maintained by a network of computers, rather than being controlled by a single person or organization.

At its most basic level, a blockchain consists of a series of blocks that are linked together in a chronological chain. Each block contains a record of one or more transactions and is secured using cryptographic techniques. Once a block has been added to the chain, it is extremely difficult to alter or remove.

For a new block to be added to the chain, it must be validated by the network. This process is known as "mining," and it involves solving a complex mathematical problem to create a new block. Once a block has been successfully mined, it is added to the chain and becomes a permanent part of the blockchain.

One of the key features of blockchain technology is its transparency. All transactions on the blockchain are visible to anyone who has access to the network, making it difficult to hide or manipulate information. This transparency is what makes blockchain technology so appealing for a variety of applications, including financial transactions, supply chain management, and voting systems.

Another key feature of blockchain technology is its security. The decentralized nature of the network, combined with the use of cryptographic techniques, makes it extremely difficult for hackers to tamper with the data on the blockchain. This makes it a highly secure platform for storing and exchanging information.

Overall, blockchain technology has the potential to revolutionize a wide range of industries by providing a secure and transparent way to track and verify transactions. It is an exciting and rapidly evolving technology that is already having a significant impact on the way we do business and exchange information.

2.3 CRYPTOCURRENCIES

Cryptocurrencies are digital or virtual currencies that use cryptography for secure financial transactions and to verify the transfer of assets. They operate on a decentralized network, meaning that they are not controlled by any single authority or organization, but are maintained by a network of computers and users.

The most well-known cryptocurrency is Bitcoin, which was created in 2009 by an unknown individual or group of individuals using the pseudonym Satoshi Nakamoto. Since its inception, Bitcoin has become the most widely used and accepted cryptocurrency and has inspired the creation of hundreds of other cryptocurrencies, known as altcoins.

Cryptocurrencies are based on blockchain technology, which is a decentralized and distributed ledger that records transactions across a network of computers. Blockchain technology uses cryptography to secure and verify transactions, making it resistant to fraud and tampering.

One of the key features of cryptocurrencies is that they are decentralized, meaning that they are not controlled by any central authority or organization. This makes them resistant to censorship and interference and allows for peer-to-peer transactions without the need for intermediaries such as banks.

Cryptocurrencies also have the potential to reduce the cost of financial transactions, as they eliminate the need for intermediaries and reduce the fees associated with traditional financial transactions. This makes them attractive for use in countries where the financial system is inefficient or unreliable, or in industries where traditional financial transactions are expensive or slow.

Cryptocurrencies have the potential to disrupt a wide range of industries, including finance, e-commerce, and remittances. They have already gained widespread adoption in some areas, such as online gambling and darknet markets, and are beginning to be accepted as a form of payment by some merchants and businesses.

Despite their potential benefits, cryptocurrencies also have significant risks and challenges. One of the main risks is the volatility of their prices, which can fluctuate significantly in a brief period. This makes cryptocurrencies risky as an investment and can make them difficult to use as a stable store of value or medium of exchange.

Another risk is the lack of regulation of the cryptocurrency market, which has led to instances of fraud, money laundering, and other illegal activities. The lack of regulation also makes it difficult for consumers to protect their rights and interests when using cryptocurrencies.

There are also questions about the scalability and sustainability of cryptocurrencies, as the energy consumption required to maintain the blockchain networks that support them has grown significantly in recent years. This has led to concerns about the environmental impact of cryptocurrencies, and the need to find ways to reduce their energy consumption.

Despite these challenges, cryptocurrencies have gained significant attention and adoption in recent years and are likely to continue to play a significant role in the future of finance and the economy. They have the potential to revolutionize the way we think about money and financial transactions and have the potential to disrupt a wide range of industries.

As the cryptocurrency market evolves and matures, it is likely that we will see the development of more sophisticated and user-friendly cryptocurrency platforms, as well as the adoption of regulatory frameworks that address the risks and challenges of cryptocurrencies. It is also likely that we will see the emergence of new applications and use cases for cryptocurrencies, as they continue to gain widespread adoption and acceptance.

2.4 WEB3

Web3, also known as the decentralized web, is the next generation of the internet in which users have more control over their data and online activities. It is a vision for a decentralized and distributed network that is built on blockchain technology and utilizes decentralized applications (dApps) that are owned and operated by the users themselves.

Web3 is a response to the centralization and privacy concerns that have emerged with the current model of the internet, known as web2. In the web2 model, a small number of large companies, such as Google, Facebook, and Amazon, have a significant amount of control over the data and activities of users. These companies often use this data for targeted advertising and have been criticized for their lack of transparency and failure to protect user privacy.

Web3 aims to address these issues by creating a decentralized network in which users have more control over their data and online activities. It utilizes blockchain technology, which is a decentralized, distributed ledger that allows for the secure, transparent, and verifiable transfer of value and information. Web3 also utilizes decentralized applications, or dApps, which are applications that run on a decentralized network and are owned and operated by the users themselves.

One of the main benefits of web3 is that it allows for the creation of a more open and decentralized internet. In the web2 model, a small number of large companies control much of the content and services that are available online. In contrast, web3 allows for the creation of dApps that are owned and operated by the users themselves, which can lead to a more diverse and open internet.

Another benefit of web3 is that it allows for increased privacy and security for users. In the web2 model, user data is often collected and used for targeted advertising, and there have been numerous instances of data breaches and cyber-attacks. Web3 utilizes blockchain technology, which allows for the secure and verifiable transfer of data and value. This can help to protect user privacy and reduce the risk of data breaches and cyber-attacks.

Web3 is still in its initial stages of development, and there are a number of challenges and issues that need to be addressed for it to reach its full potential. One of the main challenges is the lack of adoption and mainstream awareness of web3 technologies. While there are a growing number of dApps and projects that are utilizing web3 technologies, they are still a small percentage of the overall internet landscape.

Another challenge is the lack of scalability of current web3 technologies. Many current web3 projects and dApps are still limited in their ability to manage a large number of users and transactions, which can limit their potential adoption and impact.

Despite these challenges, web3 has the potential to significantly change the way we use the internet and interact with each other online. It has the potential to create a more open, decentralized, and secure internet that is owned and operated by the users themselves. As the technology and infrastructure surrounding web3 continues to develop, it will be interesting to see how it evolves and shapes the future of the internet.

2.5 METAVERSE

The concept of the metaverse has been around for decades, but in recent years it has gained renewed attention as a potential future for the internet. The metaverse is a virtual reality world that exists in parallel to the physical world and allows users to interact with each other and with virtual objects and environments in a seamless and immersive way.

The metaverse is often described as a combination of virtual reality, augmented reality, and the internet, and it has the potential to revolutionize the way we live, work, and interact with each other. Some proponents of the metaverse envision it as a vast, interconnected world where people can live, work, and play in virtual space, while others see it as a tool for enhancing the physical world by overlaying virtual information and experiences onto the real world.

One of the key features of the metaverse is that it is a shared, immersive experience that allows people to interact with each other and with virtual objects and environments in real-time. This means that users can communicate with each other and with virtual entities as if they were in the same physical space, even if they are physically located in various parts of the world.

The metaverse also has the potential to blur the lines between the physical and digital worlds, as it allows people to create and experience virtual objects and environments that are indistinguishable from the real world. This could enable people to experience things that are not possible in the physical world, such as traveling to distant planets or visiting virtual worlds with fantastical landscapes and creatures.

The metaverse has the potential to transform many aspects of our lives, including the way we work, the way we learn, and the way we entertain ourselves. For example, the metaverse could enable people to work together on virtual projects as if they were in the same physical location, even if they are scattered across the globe. It could also provide a new platform for online education, allowing students to interact with virtual instructors and each other in immersive and interactive ways.

Another potential use of the metaverse is as a platform for entertainment and leisure. The metaverse could provide a new platform for video games, movies, and other forms of media, enabling people to experience them in a fully immersive and interactive way. It could also provide a new venue for live events, such as concerts and sports games, allowing people to experience them as if they were physically present.

The development of the metaverse is still in its early stages, and there are many challenges and obstacles to overcome before it becomes a reality. One of the biggest challenges is the technical infrastructure required to support the metaverse, including the development of high-bandwidth networks, powerful computers, and advanced virtual reality hardware.

Another challenge is the creation of virtual content and experiences that are engaging, immersive, and believable. This requires the development of advanced virtual reality technologies, as well as the creation of new forms of storytelling and content creation.

There are also questions about the social and economic implications of the metaverse, including issues related to privacy, security, and the ownership and control of virtual assets. These issues will need to be addressed as the metaverse evolves, and will require the development of new laws, regulations, and governance frameworks.

Despite these challenges, the potential benefits of the metaverse are enormous, and many experts believe that it is only a matter of time before it becomes a reality. Some even predict that the metaverse will eventually become the dominant platform for human interaction and communication, replacing the physical world as the primary venue for human activity.

Whether or not this prediction comes true remains to be seen, but one thing is certain: the metaverse represents a major shift in the way we think about the internet, and it has the potential to revolutionize the world as we know it.

3 Which other technologies besides web3 and NFT are built on blockchain?

There are many technologies that are built on blockchain technology, including:

- Cryptocurrencies: These are digital currencies that use blockchain technology to secure and verify transactions. Some examples include Bitcoin, Ethereum, and Litecoin.

- Supply chain management: Blockchain technology can be used to track the movement of goods through the supply chain, improving efficiency and reducing the risk of fraud.

- Identity verification: Blockchain technology can be used to securely store and verify identity information, making it useful for applications such as voting systems and passport verification.

- Healthcare: Blockchain technology can be used to securely store and share medical records, reducing the risk of errors and improving the efficiency of the healthcare system.

- Real estate: Blockchain technology can be used to track ownership and transfer of property, simplifying the process of buying and selling real estate.

- Predictive analytics: Blockchain technology can be used to store and analyze copious amounts of data, making it useful for applications such as predicting market trends and customer behavior.

- Energy trading: Blockchain technology can be used to track and verify the production and consumption of renewable energy, enabling the creation of decentralized energy markets.

Charity: Blockchain technology can be used to track and verify charitable donations, improving transparency and accountability in the charitable sector.

4 HOW IS CREATED A CRYPTOCURRENCY

Creating a cryptocurrency is a complex process that requires a deep understanding of computer science, cryptography, and the principles of decentralized systems. It involves developing a blockchain platform and writing the code for the cryptocurrency, as well as creating a network of computers to support the cryptocurrency and verify transactions.

To create a cryptocurrency, one will typically need to have a strong background in computer science and programming, as well as a deep understanding of cryptography and decentralized systems. It is also helpful to have experience with financial concepts and markets, as many cryptocurrencies are intended to be used as a medium of exchange or store of value.

There are several steps involved in creating a cryptocurrency:

1. Define the purpose and goals of the cryptocurrency: This involves determining what problem the cryptocurrency is intended to solve, and what features it will have. This could include defining the monetary policy, transaction processing capabilities, and other features of the cryptocurrency.

2. Develop a blockchain platform: This involves creating a decentralized network of computers that will support the cryptocurrency and verify transactions. The blockchain platform should be designed to be secure, efficient, and scalable.

3. Write the code for the cryptocurrency: This involves creating the algorithms and protocols that will govern the operation of the cryptocurrency,

including the rules for creating and distributing new units of the cryptocurrency, and the mechanisms for verifying and validating transactions.

4. Launch the cryptocurrency: This involves releasing the cryptocurrency and creating a network of users and miners who will support and maintain the cryptocurrency. This may involve marketing efforts to attract users and create awareness of the cryptocurrency.

Creating a cryptocurrency is a complex and time-consuming process, and it requires a deep understanding of computer science, cryptography, and decentralized systems. It is typically not a task that can be undertaken by an individual but requires a team of experts with expertise in these areas.

Once a cryptocurrency has been created, it can be traded on cryptocurrency exchanges and used to buy and sell goods and services. However, it is important to note that the success of a cryptocurrency depends on a variety of factors, including its usefulness and usefulness, the level of adoption and acceptance it receives, and the overall state of the cryptocurrency market.

5 WHAT IS THE DIFFERENCE BETWEEN BITCOIN, ETHEREUM AND NFT?

Bitcoin, Ethereum, and non-fungible tokens (NFTs) are all related to the world of cryptocurrency and blockchain technology, but they have some significant differences.

Bitcoin is a decentralized digital currency that was created in 2009. It is the first and most well-known cryptocurrency, and it uses a decentralized ledger technology called the blockchain to record transactions. Bitcoin is based on a proof-of-work consensus algorithm, which means that miners use their computing power to solve complex mathematical problems to validate transactions and add them to the blockchain. Bitcoin is primarily used as a store of value and a medium of exchange, and it is widely accepted as a form of payment by merchants around the world.

Ethereum is a decentralized platform that runs smart contracts: applications that run exactly as programmed without any possibility of downtime, censorship, fraud, or third-party interference. These smart contracts are written in a programming language called Solidity, and they can be used to create a wide variety of applications, including decentralized finance (DeFi) platforms, prediction markets, and voting systems. Ethereum is based on a proof-of-work consensus algorithm, but it is planning to transition to a proof-of-stake algorithm in the future. In addition to running smart contracts, Ethereum also has its own cryptocurrency, called Ether, which is used to pay for transaction fees and other expenses on the Ethereum network.

NFTs are digital assets that are unique and cannot be exchanged for other assets on a one-to-one basis. They are often used to represent items such as digital art, collectibles, and other virtual goods, and they can be bought and sold on online marketplaces. NFTs are created using blockchain technology and are stored on a decentralized ledger, which allows for the verification of ownership and authenticity. They can be created on a variety of blockchain platforms, but Ethereum is currently the most popular choice for creating and trading NFTs.

In summary, Bitcoin is a decentralized digital currency that is used as a store of value and a medium of exchange, Ethereum is a decentralized platform that runs smart contracts and has its own cryptocurrency called Ether, and NFTs are digital assets that represent unique items and are stored on a decentralized ledger. While all three are related to the world of cryptocurrency and blockchain technology, they have distinct characteristics and uses.

6 Is investing in BitCoins safe?

Like any investment, investing in Bitcoin carries risks as well as potential rewards. It is important to carefully consider these risks before investing any of your money.

One of the main risks of investing in Bitcoin is its volatility. The price of Bitcoin has been known to fluctuate significantly over short periods of time, and it has experienced several major price spikes and crashes in the past. This makes it difficult to predict the value of Bitcoin in the future, and it means that there is a risk of losing money if the price decreases.

Another risk to consider is the lack of regulation in the cryptocurrency market. Bitcoin and other cryptocurrencies are not subject to the same level of regulation as traditional financial assets, which can make it more difficult to protect your investment. There have also been instances of fraud and other illegal activities involving Bitcoin, which can also pose a risk to investors.

It is also important to note that Bitcoin is a relatively new asset, and there is still a lot of uncertainty about its long-term prospects. Some experts believe that Bitcoin has the potential to become a widely accepted form of currency and a valuable asset, while others are more skeptical about its future.

In general, it is smart to be cautious when investing in Bitcoin or any other cryptocurrency. It is smarter to diversify your investments and not to invest more than you can afford to lose. It is also a promising idea to do your own research and carefully consider the risks before making any investment decisions.

7 NFTs IN THE CURRENT WORLD

Non-fungible tokens (NFTs) have gained significant attention in recent years to represent and trade unique digital assets, such as art, collectibles, and other virtual goods. NFTs are created using blockchain technology, which allows for the verification of ownership and authenticity, and they can be bought and sold on online marketplaces. The use of NFTs has the potential to revolutionize the way we think about and trade digital assets, and it has already sparked a new wave of creativity and innovation in the art and collectibles market.

One of the main benefits of NFTs is that they provide a way for creators to establish ownership and control over their digital creations. In the past, it has been difficult for artists and other creators to assert control over their digital works, as they can easily be copied and shared without permission.

NFTs provide a way for creators to claim ownership of their digital creations and to set the terms under which they can be used and distributed. This has the potential to open new opportunities for creators to monetize their work and to be fairly compensated for their efforts.

NFTs also have the potential to create new forms of value for collectors and other enthusiasts. In the past, the value of digital collectibles has been based on their utility or usefulness, rather than their uniqueness or rarity. NFTs provide a way for collectors to assign value to digital items based on their rarity and uniqueness, which can create new incentives for collectors to seek out and acquire rare or one-of-a-kind items. This has already led to the emergence of new markets for digital art and collectibles, and it has sparked a new wave of innovation and creativity in the art and collectibles market.

The use of NFTs is also closely tied to the world of cryptocurrencies, as many NFTs are created and traded using blockchain platforms that use cryptocurrency as a means of exchange. The most popular platform for creating and trading NFTs is Ethereum, which is a decentralized platform that uses its own cryptocurrency, called Ether, as a means of exchange. The use of cryptocurrency as a means of exchange for NFTs adds an additional layer of complexity and risk to the market, as the value of cryptocurrency can be volatile and is subject to market forces.

One of the main challenges faced by the NFT market is the issue of scalability. Many NFT marketplaces and platforms have struggled to manage the high volume of transactions and the large amount of data that is generated by the creation and trade of NFTs. This has led to delays and high transaction fees, which can make it difficult for some users to participate in the market. There is also a risk that the use of NFTs could contribute to the centralization of the art and collectibles market, as a few large marketplaces and platforms could come to dominate the market.

Despite these challenges, the use of NFTs has the potential to fundamentally change the way we think about and trade digital assets, and it has already had a significant impact on the art and collectibles market. As the market continues to evolve and mature, it will be interesting to see how the use of NFTs and cryptocurrencies continues to shape the future of the art and collectibles market.

8 How is web3 connected to NFT?

Web3 and non-fungible tokens (NFTs) are both technologies that are related to the decentralization of the internet and the emergence of the decentralized web, or web3. Web3 is a vision for a decentralized and distributed network that is built on blockchain technology and utilizes decentralized applications (dApps) that are owned and operated by the users themselves. NFTs are unique digital assets that are stored on a blockchain and can be used to represent a wide range of items, such as digital art, collectibles, gaming items, and virtual real estate.

There is a strong connection between web3 and NFTs, as both technologies are built on blockchain technology and are focused on creating a decentralized and distributed network. Blockchain technology allows for the secure, transparent, and verifiable transfer of value and information, which is essential for both web3 and NFTs.

One of the main ways that web3 and NFTs are connected is using decentralized applications, or dApps. dApps are applications that run on a decentralized network and are owned and operated by the users themselves. They can be used for a wide range of purposes, including the creation and sale of NFTs.

One of the key benefits of dApps is that they allow for the creation of unique digital assets that can be easily bought and sold. This has opened new opportunities for artists and collectors to sell and purchase digital art using NFTs and has also led to the emergence of new markets for digital collectibles and gaming items.

In addition to the use of dApps, web3 and NFTs are also connected through their focus on decentralization and the empowerment of users. In the web2 model of the internet, a small number of large companies have a significant amount of control over the data and activities of users. In contrast, web3 and NFTs allow for the creation of a more decentralized and distributed network in which users have more control over their data and online activities.

There are also a number of challenges and issues that need to be addressed for web3 and NFTs to reach their full potential. One of the main challenges is the lack of adoption and mainstream awareness of these technologies. While there are a growing number of dApps and NFTs that are utilizing web3 technologies, they are still a small percentage of the overall internet landscape.

Another challenge is the lack of scalability of current web3 and NFT technologies. Many current projects and dApps are still limited in their ability to manage a large number of users and transactions, which can limit their potential adoption and impact.

Despite these challenges, web3 and NFTs have the potential to significantly change the way we use the internet and interact with each other online. They have the potential to create a more open, decentralized, and secure internet that is owned and operated by the users themselves, and to revolutionize the way we think about digital art and collectibles. As the technology and infrastructure surrounding these technologies continues to develop, it will be interesting to see how they evolve and shape the future of the internet.

9 What are the connections between Metaverse and Blockchain?

The connection between the metaverse and blockchain technology is that blockchain can potentially be used to support and enable the development of the metaverse.

The metaverse is a virtual reality world that exists in parallel to the physical world and allows users to interact with each other and with virtual objects and environments in a seamless and immersive way. One of the key challenges in creating the metaverse is the development of a technical infrastructure that can support the high-bandwidth networks, powerful computers, and advanced virtual reality hardware needed to enable immersive and interactive virtual experiences.

Blockchain technology has the potential to play a role in addressing this challenge by supplying a decentralized and distributed platform for storing and managing data, assets, and transactions in the metaverse. By using blockchain, it may be possible to create a decentralized metaverse that is not controlled by any single entity but is supported by a network of computers and users.

Blockchain could also be used to enable the creation and exchange of virtual assets in the metaverse. For example, users could create and sell virtual real estate, art, or other virtual goods using blockchain-based smart contracts. Blockchain could also be used to ease the transfer of ownership and control of virtual assets between users, enabling the creation of a virtual economy in the metaverse.

There are also potential applications of blockchain in other areas of the metaverse, such as identity verification and reputation management. Blockchain could be used to securely store and verify identity information for users in the metaverse, as well as to track the reputation and trustworthiness of users in the virtual world.

Overall, the connection between the metaverse and blockchain is that blockchain technology has the potential to support and enable the development of the metaverse by supplying a decentralized and distributed platform for storing and managing data, assets, and transactions in the virtual world.

10 How can a piece of art be purchased?

The market for Non-Fungible Tokens (NFTs) works in an analogous way to other markets, with buyers and sellers coming together to trade NFTs. The value of an NFT is determined by a variety of factors, including the rarity and uniqueness of the digital asset, the reputation and fame of the creator, and the demand from collectors and investors.

There are a number of different platforms and exchanges that allow for the buying and selling of NFTs. Some of these platforms are specifically designed for NFTs, while others allow for the trading of a wider range of digital assets. Some examples of popular NFT platforms and exchanges include:

- OpenSea: A marketplace for buying and selling NFTs, including art, collectibles, and virtual real estate.

- Rarible: A platform for creating, buying, and selling NFTs, with a focus on art and collectibles.

- Nifty Gateway: A platform for buying and selling NFTs, including art, music, and other digital assets.

- SuperRare: A marketplace for buying and selling digital art as NFTs.

- KnownOrigin: A platform for buying and selling digital art as NFTs, with a focus on contemporary artists.

To buy or sell NFTs on these platforms, users typically need to create an account and use cryptocurrency, such as

Ethereum, to make transactions. Some platforms may also require users to go through a verification process to participate.

Overall, the NFT market is an exciting and rapidly evolving space, and there are many different platforms and exchanges available for buying and selling NFTs. However, it is important to do thorough research and due diligence before participating in the NFT market, as the value of NFTs can be highly volatile and there is always a risk of fraud or other types of misconduct.

11 WHAT DO YOU OWN PURCHASING AN NFT?

When a purchaser buys a non-fungible token (NFT), they own a unique digital asset that is recorded on a blockchain. The NFT represents ownership of the digital asset, which could be a piece of art, music, a video, a piece of virtual real estate, or any other type of digital content.

The NFT itself is a digital token that contains information about the digital asset, including a unique identifier and metadata such as the name, artist, or creator of the asset. The NFT also includes a link to the digital asset, which could be a file stored on a decentralized file storage system such as InterPlanetary File System (IPFS).

When a purchaser buys an NFT, they own the NFT itself and the rights associated with it, such as the right to display or sell the NFT. However, the purchaser does not own the copyright to the digital asset represented by the NFT. This means that the purchaser does not have the right to reproduce or distribute the asset without the permission of the copyright holder.

It is important for NFT buyers to understand the rights and limitations associated with their purchase, and to carefully review the terms and conditions of the NFT before making a purchase.

12 NFTs CAN BE CONTROLLED?

Non-Fungible Tokens (NFTs) are digital assets that use blockchain technology to prove ownership and authenticity. One of the key features of NFTs is that they are stored on a decentralized database, which means that they are not controlled by any single person or organization. This makes them resistant to censorship and allows for an elevated level of transparency and security.

However, while NFTs themselves cannot be controlled, the platforms that they are bought and sold on may have their own policies and regulations governing the use of NFTs. For example, a marketplace or exchange that allows for the buying and selling of NFTs may have rules about what types of NFTs are allowed to be traded on the platform and may also have policies in place to prevent fraud or other types of misconduct.

Additionally, while the blockchain technology that powers NFTs is highly secure, it is still possible for NFTs to be hacked or stolen if the appropriate security measures are not taken. For example, if an individual's digital wallet, which stores their NFTs, is not properly secured, it may be vulnerable to hacking or other types of cyber-attacks.

Overall, while NFTs themselves cannot be directly controlled, it is important to consider the policies and security measures in place on the platforms that they are bought and sold on, as well as the measures that individuals can take to protect their own NFTs.

13 WHAT IS THE TURNOVER SOLD ON NFT IN 2022?

It is difficult to determine the total amount of Non-Fungible Tokens (NFTs) that have been sold, as the market for NFTs is still relatively new and there is no central authority that tracks sales data. Additionally, the price of NFTs can vary significantly depending on the rarity and uniqueness of the digital asset, as well as the demand from collectors and investors.

However, it is clear that the market for NFTs has grown significantly in recent years, and there have been numerous high-profile sales of NFTs that have garnered significant attention. For example, in March 2021, an NFT artwork by the artist Beeple sold for a record-breaking $69.3 million at Christie's auction house, making it one of the most expensive NFTs ever sold.

Other notable examples of NFT sales include a tweet by the CEO of Jack Dorsey's social media platform Twitter, which sold for over $2.9 million, and a video clip from the band Kings of Leon, which sold for over $500,000.

Overall, while it is difficult to determine the total amount of NFTs that have been sold, the market for NFTs is growing and that there is significant demand for unique and rare digital assets.

14 What are the most famous NFTs about?

Non-Fungible Tokens (NFTs) can be used to represent a wide range of digital assets, including art, music, videos, and even tweets. As such, the most popular NFTs tend to vary depending on the interests and preferences of collectors and investors.

That being said, some of the most popular NFTs tend to be those that are unique, rare, or created by well-known and respected creators. For example, NFTs created by famous artists or musicians tend to be highly sought after, as do NFTs that represent one-of-a-kind or limited-edition digital items.

Some examples of popular NFTs include:

- Digital art: Digital art has become a popular category for NFTs, with many artists using NFTs to sell and showcase their work. Some of the most popular NFTs in this category are created by well-known artists such as Beeple, who has achieved significant fame and success in the NFT market.

- Music: NFTs have also been used to represent music, with some artists releasing limited edition NFTs that include exclusive tracks or other bonus content. Some of the most popular NFTs in this category have been created by high-profile artists such as Kings of Leon and Linkin Park.

- Collectible games: NFTs have also been used in the creation of collectible games, such as CryptoKitties, which allows players to breed, collect, and trade unique digital cats. These types of NFTs tend to be popular with collectors and gamers alike.

- Memes and social media: NFTs have also been used to represent memes and other types of social media content, with some NFTs selling for significant sums of money. For example, a tweet by the CEO of Jack Dorsey's social media platform Twitter sold for over $2.9 million.

Overall, the most popular NFTs tend to be those that are unique, rare, or created by well-known and respected creators, and which represent digital assets that are in high demand.

15 How does CryptoKitties work?

CryptoKitties is a popular online game that allows players to breed, collect, and trade unique digital cats. The game was launched in 2017 on the Ethereum blockchain, and it quickly gained a large and devoted following.

CryptoKitties became famous for being one of the first mainstream uses of Non-Fungible Tokens (NFTs), which are digital assets that use blockchain technology to prove ownership and authenticity. In the game, each CryptoKitty is a unique NFT, and players can buy, sell, and trade them using cryptocurrency.

The value of a CryptoKitty is determined by a variety of factors, including its rarity and uniqueness, as well as its genetic traits, which are passed down from one generation to the next. Some of the rarest and most valuable CryptoKitties have sold for hundreds of thousands of dollars, making them some of the most valuable NFTs in the world.

In addition to being a popular and lucrative game, CryptoKitties also helped to bring attention and mainstream acceptance to the concept of NFTs and blockchain technology. It demonstrated the potential for NFTs to be used to own and trade unique digital items, and it paved the way for the development of other NFT-based games and applications.

Overall, CryptoKitties is famous for being a pioneer in the world of NFTs and for its enduring popularity as a collectible and trading game.

16 The environmental impact of NFTs

The environmental impact of non-fungible tokens (NFTs) has been a topic of debate in recent years, as the energy consumption associated with the creation and trade of NFTs has come under scrutiny. NFTs are created using blockchain technology, which requires a significant amount of energy to power the computers and servers that process and validate transactions. This has led to concerns about the environmental impact of NFTs and the sustainability of the NFT market.

One of the main sources of energy consumption in the NFT market is the process of mining, which is used to create new blocks on the blockchain and to validate transactions. Mining requires powerful computers and servers to solve complex mathematical problems, which can be energy intensive. The energy consumption of mining varies depending on the blockchain platform and the type of mining equipment used, but it is generally higher for proof-of-work (PoW) blockchain platforms, such as Ethereum, which is the most popular platform for creating and trading NFTs.

The energy consumption of the NFT market has been the subject of significant controversy, as the important levels of energy consumption have been criticized as being unsustainable and contributing to climate change. Some experts have called for more sustainable alternatives to PoW mining, such as proof-of-stake (PoS) algorithms, which are less energy-intensive and rely on a different mechanism for validating transactions. Ethereum has announced plans to transition to a PoS algorithm in the future, which could help to reduce the energy consumption of the NFT market.

Another concern related to the environmental impact of NFTs is the carbon footprint of the NFT market. The energy consumption of the NFT market generates greenhouse gases, which contribute to climate change. The carbon footprint of the NFT market is difficult to quantify, as it depends on the mix of energy sources used to power the mining process and the efficiency of the mining equipment. However, some estimates have suggested that the carbon footprint of the NFT market could be significant, depending on the assumptions used.

There have also been efforts to address the environmental impact of NFTs by renewable energy sources and carbon offsetting. Some NFT marketplaces and platforms have committed to using renewable energy sources to power their operations, and some have implemented carbon offsetting programs to mitigate their carbon emissions. These efforts could help to reduce the environmental impact of the NFT market and make it more sustainable in the long term.

In summary, the environmental impact of NFTs has been a topic of debate, as the energy consumption and carbon emissions associated with the creation and trade of NFTs have raised concerns about the sustainability of the NFT market. Efforts to reduce the energy consumption and carbon footprint of the NFT market, such as the use of renewable energy sources and carbon offsetting, could help to address these concerns and make the NFT market more sustainable in the long term.

17 CAN NFT BE A WAY TO CONTRAST THE ILLEGAL MARKET?

Non-fungible tokens (NFTs) have the potential to play a role in combating illegal market activity, as they provide a way to establish ownership and authenticity for digital assets. Illegal market activity, such as counterfeiting and illicit trade, can undermine the value and integrity of genuine products and harm consumers, producers, and the overall economy. The use of NFTs can help to combat illegal market activity by providing a way to establish the provenance and authenticity of digital assets and to track their ownership and movement.

One way in which NFTs can be used to combat illegal market activity is by providing a way to verify the authenticity of digital art and collectibles. Counterfeiting and the sale of fake or knock-off items is a major problem in the art and collectibles market, and it can erode the value and reputation of genuine items. By using NFTs to establish the ownership and authenticity of digital art and collectibles, it becomes much more difficult for counterfeiters to produce and sell fake items. NFTs also provide a way for collectors and other enthusiasts to verify the authenticity of the items they are purchasing, which can help to protect them from being duped by counterfeiters.

NFTs can also be used to combat illegal market activity in the trade of physical items, such as luxury goods and endangered species. The use of NFTs can help to establish the provenance and authenticity of these items, which can make it more difficult for illegal traders to produce and sell fake or illicit items. By tracking the ownership and movement of these items using NFTs, it becomes easier to identify and prosecute illegal traders and to protect the value and integrity of genuine products.

The use of NFTs can also help to combat illegal market activity in the online marketplace. The anonymity of the internet and the lack of physical verification make it easier for illegal traders to sell fake or illicit items online. By using NFTs to verify the ownership and authenticity of items, it becomes much more difficult for illegal traders to operate in the online marketplace. NFTs can also provide a way for law enforcement agencies to trace the ownership and movement of illegal items and to identify and prosecute illegal traders.

In summary, the use of NFTs has the potential to play a role in combating illegal market activity by providing a way to establish ownership and authenticity for digital assets. By verifying the provenance and authenticity of items, NFTs can make it more difficult for counterfeiters and illegal traders to operate and can help to protect the value and integrity of genuine products. The use of NFTs can also help to trace the ownership and movement of illegal items and to identify and prosecute illegal traders, which can help to deter illegal market activity and protect consumers and producers.

18 CAN ANYBODY CREATE AN NFT?

In general, anyone can create a non-fungible token (NFT) as long as they have the necessary technical skills and resources. NFTs are created using blockchain technology, which requires a certain level of familiarity with programming and cryptography.

To create an NFT, you will need to follow a few steps:

- Choose a blockchain platform that supports the creation of NFTs. Some popular options include Ethereum, EOS, and TRON.

- Familiarize yourself with the technical requirements and limitations of the chosen platform. This may include learning about smart contracts and the programming language used to create them.

- Create the NFT itself, which typically involves creating a digital file and assigning it a unique identifier on the blockchain.

- Publish the NFT on a marketplace or platform that allows you to sell it to others.

It is important to note that creating an NFT is not an effortless process, and it may require a significant amount of time and resources to learn the necessary skills and create a successful NFT. Additionally, the value of an NFT is largely determined by the demand for it, so it is important to consider the market and the potential audience for your NFT before creating and selling it.

19 CAN NFT BE A WAY TO EARN?

It is possible to earn income from selling non-fungible tokens (NFTs) as a side hustle. NFTs are digital assets that are unique and cannot be exchanged for other assets on a one-to-one basis. They are often used to represent items such as digital art, collectibles, and other virtual goods and can be bought and sold on online marketplaces.

If you have a talent for creating digital art or other types of content that can be represented as an NFT, you may be able to sell your NFTs on online marketplaces and earn income from them. There are also other ways to earn income from NFTs, such as by creating and selling your own NFT marketplace or by curating a collection of NFTs and reselling them.

It is important to note that the market for NFTs is still relatively new and can be volatile, so it is important to do your research and be aware of the risks before getting involved. It is also a clever idea to diversify your investments and not rely on NFTs as your sole source of income.

20 NFT AND TAXATION

The taxation of non-fungible tokens (NFTs) has become a subject of increasing interest as the market for NFTs has grown and evolved. NFTs are digital assets that are unique and cannot be exchanged for other assets on a one-to-one basis, and they are often used to represent items such as digital art, collectibles, and other virtual goods. The taxation of NFTs can be complex and depends on the specific circumstances and legal jurisdiction involved.

In general, the taxation of NFTs is like the taxation of other types of digital assets and depends on the nature of the NFT and how it is used. In the United States, for example, the Internal Revenue Service (IRS) has issued guidance on the taxation of NFTs, stating that the sale or exchange of NFTs is generally taxable by law. The tax treatment of NFTs is based on whether they are classified as a capital asset, such as a stock or a bond, or as a collectible, such as art or a rare coin. Capital assets are taxed at a lower rate than collectibles, and the tax treatment of NFTs will depend on which category they fall into.

The taxation of NFTs also depends on the purpose for which they are being used. If an NFT is being used as a medium of exchange, such as for buying and selling goods and services, it may be subject to sales tax or value-added tax (VAT). If an NFT is being used as a store of value, such as for investment purposes, it may be subject to capital gains tax or other tax rules depending on the jurisdiction.

The taxation of NFTs can also be affected by the country or jurisdiction in which they are being traded or used. Some countries have adopted specific tax rules for NFTs, while others have yet to address the taxation of NFTs in their tax laws. This can create uncertainty and complexity for NFT traders and investors, as they may be subject to different tax rules depending on where they are located and where the NFTs are being traded.

One of the main challenges faced by the NFT market regarding taxation is the lack of clarity and consistency in the tax treatment of NFTs. The rapid pace of innovation and change in the NFT market has made it difficult for tax authorities to keep up with the developments and to provide clear guidance on the tax treatment of NFTs. This has led to confusion and uncertainty for NFT traders and investors, who may be uncertain about their tax obligations and how to comply with the relevant tax rules.

To address these challenges, it will be important for tax authorities to provide clear guidance on the taxation of NFTs and to consider the unique characteristics of NFTs and the specific circumstances in which they are being used. This could involve adopting specific tax rules for NFTs or providing guidance on how existing tax rules should be applied to NFTs. It will also be important for NFT traders and investors to be aware of the tax rules that apply to NFTs and to seek professional advice as needed to ensure compliance with the relevant tax laws.

In summary, the taxation of NFTs is a complex and evolving area, and it depends on the nature of the NFT and how it is being used. To address the challenges faced by the NFT market about taxation, it will be important for tax authorities to provide clear guidance on the tax treatment of NFTs and for NFT traders and investors to be aware of the relevant tax rules and to seek professional advice as needed.

21 QUANTUM, THE WORLD'S FIRST NFT

Quantum is the world's first non-fungible token, or NFT, which was created in 2017 by Matt Hall and John Watkinson. Quantum was created to authenticate and sell digital art, and it gained significant attention and popularity within the cryptocurrency and art communities.

Quantum was sold in a live auction for Ethereum, with the winning bid of 24,000 Ether (worth around $17.5 million at the time). Since its creation, Quantum has become a highly sought-after and valuable digital asset, and it has helped to establish the use of NFTs to authenticate and sell unique digital art.

In addition to its value as a digital asset, Quantum has also gained a reputation as a pioneering work of art. It has been exhibited in galleries and museums around the world and has been featured in numerous articles and interviews.

Overall, Quantum has played a significant role in the development and popularization of NFTs, and it continues to be a highly influential and important work within the world of digital art and cryptocurrency.

22 What are the most common frauds about NFTs and how to get protected?

There are several common frauds that have been reported in the non-fungible token (NFT) market. Here are a few examples:

Fake NFTs: Some scammers create and sell NFTs that are not genuine or have little value. These fake NFTs may be copies of existing NFTs or completely new creations that are presented as valuable or rare. To protect yourself from this fraud, do your research before buying an NFT. Look for reputable sellers and verify the authenticity and value of the NFT before making a purchase.

Phishing attacks: Some scammers use phishing attacks to trick people into giving away their private keys or login credentials. To protect yourself from this fraud, be wary of any links or messages that ask you to enter your private key or login information, and only enter this information on trusted websites.

Ponzi schemes: Some scammers use NFTs as part of a Ponzi scheme, where early investors are paid returns with the money from later investors. These schemes are not sustainable and will eventually collapse, leaving many investors with significant losses. To protect yourself from this fraud, be cautious of any investments that promise unrealistic returns or that rely on a constant influx of new investors to pay out earlier investors.

Fraudulent sales: Some scammers create fake NFTs or fraudulently sell NFTs that they do not own. To protect yourself from this fraud, verify the ownership and authenticity of an NFT before making a purchase.

To protect yourself from NFT frauds, it is important to do your research and be cautious when making a purchase. Be sure to only buy NFTs from reputable sellers and verify the authenticity and value of the NFT before making a purchase. It is also a clever idea to familiarize yourself with the risks and potential frauds in the NFT market.

23 JOHN TAVERN - THE AUTHOR

John Tavern is a highly respected expert in the field of cryptocurrencies and non-fungible tokens (NFTs). He has been involved in the cryptocurrency industry for over a decade and has a deep understanding of the technical and financial aspects of this rapidly evolving market.

John's background is in computer science and finance, and he has a master's degree in both fields from a top-tier university. He has worked as a software engineer at several leading technology companies and has also held senior positions in the finance industry, where he has gained extensive experience in financial analysis and risk management.

In recent years, John has become particularly interested in NFTs, and has become a leading authority on this emerging technology. He has authored numerous articles and papers on NFTs and has given numerous talks and presentations on the subject at conferences and events around the world.

In addition to his work in the cryptocurrency and NFT industries, John is also an active member of several online communities and forums related to these topics. He is known for his thoughtful and insightful contributions and is widely respected for his expertise and knowledge.

In his spare time, John enjoys reading, writing, and exploring the outdoors. He is also an avid collector of NFTs and has built up a significant collection of rare and valuable NFTs over the years.

Overall, John is a highly knowledgeable and respected expert in the fields of cryptocurrencies and NFTs and is well-known for his contributions to these industries. His background in computer science and finance, combined with his deep understanding of the technical and financial aspects of these technologies, make him an asset to any team or organization working in these fields.

24 TABLE OF CONTENT

1 Preface 2

2 Definitions: 4

   2.1   NFTs 4

   2.2   Blockchain 7

   2.3   Cryptocurrencies 9

   2.4   Web3 13

   2.5   Metaverse 17

3 Which other technologies besides web3 and NFT are built on blockchain? 23

4 How is created a cryptocurrency 26

5 What is the difference between BITCOIN, ETHEREUM and NFT? 30

6 Is investing in BitCoins safe? 34

7 NFTs in the current world 37

8 How is web3 connected to NFT? 41

9 What are the connections between Metaverse and Blockchain? 45

10	How can a piece of art be purchased?........................48
11	What do you own purchasing an NFT?......................51
12	NFTs can be controlled?..53
13	What is the turnover sold on NFT in 2022?................55
14	What are the most famous NFTs about?......................57
15	How does CryptoKitties work? 60
16	The environmental impact of NFTs.............................62
17	Can NFT be a way to contrast the illegal market?....66
18	Can anybody create an NFT? 70
19	Can NFT be a way to earn?..72
20	NFT and taxation 74
21	Quantum, the world's first NFT 78
22	What are the most common frauds about NFTs and how to get protected? 80
23	John Tavern - The Author..83

www.ingramcontent.com/pod-product-compliance
Lightning Source LLC
Chambersburg PA
CBHW070300220526
45465CB00004B/1682